Praise for *From This Purple Chair to Yours*

Ripples is inspiring to me. In the middle of this chaotic world, I've realized how often I forget to pause, ponder, and pray. The busyness of life steals away those moments that are meant to refresh my soul. Ripples from *The Purple Chair* is a sweet reminder of what God truly wants for me—to step into His peace and simply dwell with Him, even if only for a moment.

—Marcia Botts, Tennessee

This book spoke to my spirit—my inner being—The Ripple Book helped me to Pause, Relax, Renew my mind, Reignite within my soul—my first love—my Creator, who knows me inside and out, from before my first breath to my last! Yet, I am His Beloved.

—Debbie Honeycutt, North Carolina

Kathy Emeigh's book *From This Purple Chair to Yours: Ripples of Pause, Ponder, and Prayer* is a gem. Her relatable thoughts resonate with me and inspire me to rest in my "purple chair," which is really one that is blue and white.

The book's format is so easy to read, and it prods me to sit back and pause to think how this all relates to me and my life, and it reminds me how God is right beside me whenever I need Him and He can handle all my problems better than I can.

—Mary Ann Eichenlaub, South Carolina

From This Purple Chair to Yours is a well-written, easy-to-follow book for working through thoughts or issues that are negatively impacting your life. Several aspects of *This Purple Chair* resonated with me personally. I appreciated the word pictures that Kathy evoked for negative thoughts. I could visualize them as she presented them and imagine them disappearing as you work through the suggested Pause and journaling activities. I thought the Journal Invitation was a great way to word the journal exercise as it did not feel like a demand/must, which, for me, is much more doable. In addition, I thought the Journal Invitation and Pause activities were proactive, simple exercises for moving towards inner peace.

And I hope that the readers of this book will find in their hearts/humanity their ability to love and care for each other regardless of differences.

—KM, Pennsylvania

Kathy Emeigh's *From This Purple Chair to Yours: Ripples of Pause, Ponder and Prayer* offers a gentle, persistent invitation to healing—calling us to ponder the contrast between our human struggle and the Holy God who calls us by name. The text bids you to step out of your busy life, to find your own "purple chair" (her metaphor for a quiet corner), and to answer questions that, by their very nature, invite deep reflection. For those new to pausing and prayer, Kathy's warm and encouraging words will lead you into stillness with the Holy One. Each ripple concludes with a prayer and journal prompt to help you carry that stillness into your daily life. Enjoy becoming a ripple of peace, stillness, and love in a world that deeply needs it—alone, with a friend, or in a small group.

—Kim Denyes, MATS, Spiritual Director

From
This Purple Chair
To Yours

From
This Purple Chair
To Yours

Ripples of Pause,
Ponder, and Prayer

Kathy Suess Emeigh

Cover and interior design by Kathy Emeigh.
Front cover photo by Janet Pressler.
ISBN 979-8-89420-073-6
Library of Congress Control Number 2025925659
See page 91 for Scripture references and acknowledgments

For more information or to place bulk orders, contact the author or the publisher at Jennifer@BrightCommunications.net.

Bright
COMMUNICATIONS

Compelled by *The One Who calls me beloved,*

To sit in This Purple Chair

And pause, ponder, and pray and write to you,

For you are

Uniquely, elegantly, and exquisitely created to be you,

By the Designer of all designers.

Take that in and Breathe ...

This Purple Chair

Kathy Emeigh

Ripples

Preface

This book is not only mine; it is yours.

Though I penned these words, they come alive only when they meet *your* story, *your* breath, *your* longing, *your* discovering, and *your* becoming.

As you lean into these pages, you become the author of your own whole self—your essence, your earth suit, your thoughts, your choices, and the ways you will ripple out into your corner of the world.

Why Ripples?

I call each reflection a ripple because **we are a ripple**, living vessels of energy, movement, and love.

We are our essence—uniquely, exquisitely and elegantly made—beloved of the Beloved. Our essence was crafted and breathed into by the love of the Beloved.

And at just the right time, we were woven together in the womb and clothed in an earth suit.

Essence and Earth suit. One.

As we journey through life, we sometimes become a little off balance—too much earth suit and not enough essence.

The invitation of life is to grow into our whole self: body and soul, humanity and divinity, seen and unseen.

And so, when that wholeness begins to flow out, we send ripples into our corners of the world—

gently, powerful waves of being. Every thought, word, act becomes part of the current that moves through creation. And like ripples in a lake, even the smallest ones travel far beyond what we can see.

The Structure of a Ripple

Each ripple in this book follows a sacred rhythm, an intentional flow for the soul's unfolding.

1. Gather

Before we can reflect, we must intentionally arrive. In this space, we quiet the mind, slow the swirl, and let the "snow globe" of our thoughts settle. Scripture and sacred words invite us to gather our scattered pieces and be still.

2. Reflecting the Human Struggle

Here we look gently and honestly at our humanity—our aches and imperfections, our doubts and desires. We acknowledge that life can be hard, chaotic, and that our earth suits can grow weary.

3. Illumined by the Divine Contrast

But the story never ends with the struggle. There is always more to see, to hear, to understand, to be inspired by.

Here we turn our faces toward the Light that illumines our path toward love, truth, wisdom, hope, faith...clarity and coherence.

This is the moment where your essence rises and your earth suit softens. We begin to see our lives through the lens of Divine possibility.

4. Pause & Ponder

This is a place to linger, wonder, breathe, and be. This is a sacred place, an invitation to hear the message as it settles in our hearts. For me, this is a place of curiosity, safety and peace. It is spacious.

A Little Note on the Ampersand (&)

The ampersand is one of my favorite symbols because it reminds me:

There is always more in the mystery and ways of The Divine.

More grace.

More wisdom.

More becoming.

More love waiting to be revealed.

More.

---

5. Prayer & Journal Invitation

Here we respond. Letting our hearts speak, we let our pens move. We let our essence give shape to what is stirring within us.

Prayer becomes real.

Journaling becomes authorship.

Stillness becomes guidance.

This is the moment where each ripple becomes yours and mine—personal, intimate, and uniquely shaped by our journeys.

6. Proceed...

We have intentionally come here. And now we rise and go forth. We proceed. We return to our corners of the world. Encouraged. Changed. Carrying new awarenesses, growing in love and wisdom and peace. We extend these gifts to all we meet today.

Enjoy your journey. It is exciting and life-changing, and you won't be disappointed.

A Gentle Introduction

There's a chair in the corner of my room—quiet, purple, well-worn—where candles flicker, the fountain bubbles, and I come to sit. Not to fix. Not to strive. Just to pause ... to ponder ... to pray. This purple chair has become a sanctuary: a sacred space where I return to what is most true.

Here, I bring all of me. The wonky and the wondering. The anxious and the aching. The clarity and the chaos. I don't always arrive in peace, but I come with a willingness—to breathe, to be still, and to listen again to the deeper voice.

The Divine whisper that gently reminds me:

You are seen.

You are loved.

You are not alone.

These ripples of pause, ponder, and prayer were born right here in this purple chair—from moments of stillness, surprise, and sacred surrender. Each ripple flows from a space of awareness and deep invitation. They are not polished answers but reflections—gentle guides to help you sit with your own thoughts and longings and to discover the Divine Contrast that brings peace in the midst of your human experience.

So come. Sit with me.

Bring your coffee, your journal, your tears, your questions. Bring your joy, your fatigue, your regrets, your hope.

Bring your true self.

All of you belongs.

Let this purple chair—or whatever chair is yours—be a resting place. A returning place. A sacred space where you remember:

Remember:

-You are uniquely, exquisitely, and elegantly designed.

-You are beloved.

-And you carry ripples that will touch the world.

Pause.

Ponder.

Pray.

And ripple outward, for such a time as this.

A cozy, cozy moment begins.

The Meta-Ripple

Brimming Over with Hope

Gather

Now may the God of hope fill you with all joy and peace in believing, so that you may abound in hope by the power of the Holy Spirit.

— Romans 15:13 (NASB)

Oh! May the God of green hope fill you up with joy, fill you up with peace, so that your believing lives, filled with the life giving energy of the Holy Spirit may brim over with Hope!

— Romans 15:13 (MSG)

Reflecting on the Human Struggle

We search so hard for joy and peace, don't we? We chase them in objects and achievements— things that rust and rot and break down. And yet, the more we collect, sometimes the more depleted we feel.

That darn "if only..." voice.

- If only I had more...
- If only things were different...
- If only I were more... then joy would come, peace would settle in, hope would bloom.

We forget that joy and peace do not come to us from the outside. They bloom within, especially when we examine the stories we believe. So many of our thoughts are decades old—unchallenged, on repeat.

What we believe feels like truth... until we pause, hold the belief with compassion, and gently ask:

- How does this thought make me feel?
- What does it do to my body?
- What behaviors follow in its wake?

Illumined by the Divine Contrast

Romans 15:13 speaks of a believing life that brims over with hope—not from willpower, but from the power of the Holy Spirit.

This is not about believing harder, but believing differently. It's not about ignoring our old thoughts, but sitting with them, gently, in the lap of love. It's not sitting not with judgment, but with (TLC^3): Tender Loving Care, Compassion, and Curiosity.

We come to this purple chair.

We sit in the liminal space, between the old belief that drains and the new truth that fills.

We breathe there.

We begin again here.

Pause & Ponder

In the stillness of your own purple chair, ask:

- What thought have I carried for decades without question?
- Is it stealing joy? Blocking peace?
- What might a Spirit-breathed, life-giving thought sound like instead?

Try it on.

See how it feels in your body.

Notice what shifts in your emotions... your breath... your next step.

Prayer

God of green hope, fill me today with joy and peace not because everything is right, but because I believe differently.

Transform my inner thought-landscape and teach my mind to rest in what is true, kind, life-giving, and eternal.

May I brim over with hope—rooted, rising, and radiant—by the power of Your Spirit. May I ripple out to my corner of the world and beyond...

Amen & Amen.

Journal Invitation

Write an old, repeated belief that's been guiding your reactions or choices. Then rewrite it in the voice of hope, joy, peace, and the Holy Spirit. Let your new belief become your new ripple.

Proceed...

Ripple 1

Reclaiming the Director's Chair of My Perspectives, My Thoughts

Gather

Bring your thought into the same trusting posture Jesus lived in.

> — paraphrase of 2 Corinthians 10:5b

Do not be anxious about anything, but in every situation, by prayer and petition, with thanksgiving, present your requests to God and the Peace of God, which transcends all understanding, will guard your hearts and minds in Christ Jesus. Finally...whatever is true, noble, right, pure, lovely, admirable—if any thing is excellent or praiseworthy think about such things.

> — Philippians 4:6,8

Reflecting on the Human Struggle

For a long time, I believed my thoughts ruled me. That I was helpless in their grip. That they were my fault. That they meant something about me—something shameful or weak or broken.

But I now know something different. Thoughts are physical structures in the brain. They form from messages I've heard—from those who loved me, those who didn't, and those who didn't know how. They're shaped by society, fear, trauma, the substances I used to numb the pain... and even by my own overthinking.

And sometimes? They just get stuck.

My earth suit is sticky. Thoughts attach. They swirl. They spiral. They cyclone.

Illumined by the Divine Contrast

But—and—there is a Divine Perspective. There is a choice.

"Choose this day..."

Not between heaven or hell—

But between toxic thinking and life-giving thought.

Between 'shame storms' and 'sacred stillness.'

Between condemnation and curiosity.

Between old perspectives and new perspectives.

Between the stimulus and reaction.

When I **pause,**

When I enter the **liminal space**, the in-between space.

When I breathe and become aware of my thoughts without judgment, I reclaim my role.

I sit down in the **director's chair** of my thought life, and I *choose* the thinking that I want to live into.

It doesn't happen overnight. But transformation does come. The ruts get softer. The new paths get clearer. The brain rewires.

And peace? That peace, that surpasses all understanding?

That peace ripples out—from me to others, to my world, and even to the thoughts I used to fear.

Pause & Ponder

- What thoughts feel sticky to me right now?
- Have I been operating as if they have power over me?
- What would it feel like to gently notice them with compassion instead of shame?
- Can I pause, breathe, and step into the director's chair of my thought life?
- What new thought might I choose to write in today's scene?

Prayer

God of awareness and grace,

Thank you for the miracle of thought—and the freedom to choose.

Help me pause.

Help me notice.

Help me release the thoughts that no longer serve me.

With TLC[3] (Tender Loving Care, Compassion, and Curiosity).

Let me write new ones—rooted in truth, love, and hope.

May my inner ripples become outer ones,

As I sit—awake and willing—in the director's chair of my thoughts. Listening for You.

Amen & Amen

Journal Invitation

What thought do I most need to reframe today—with love?

(And NOT with condemnation, judgment, guilt, shame, blame, regret...)

_____

_____

_____

_____

Proceed...

Ripple 2

Uniquely, Exquisitely, and Elegantly Designed (a.k.a. the "gem")

Gather

God saw all that he had made, and it was very good.

— Genesis 1:31

I praise you because I am fearfully and wonderfully made; your works are wonderful, I know that full well.

— Psalm 139:14 (NIV 1984)

Reflecting on the Human Struggle

Sometimes we forget;

Forget who we are.

Forget who others are.

Forget that before we were broken, we were beautiful.

Before the world wounded us, we were wonderfully made.

In a world filled with labels, judgments, and hasty conclusions, we overlook the deep truth:

No one else has ever been created like you.

Or like that stranger. Or the one who frustrates you. Or the one you love. Each one of us is unique, exquisite, and elegantly designed.

In moments of irritation or indifference, with ourselves or others, it's easy to forget that we are beholding a living gem—someone *very good* in God's original design.

Illumined by The Divine Contrast

The animals were good.

The mountains were good.

The oceans, the skies, the trees—all good.

But then God made humankind... and He said: *very good*...a "gem."

He breathed into humanity something different—the Imago Dei.

And into that Divine design, He placed the need for connection—for a partner suitable, equally crafted in beauty and intention.

You were not mass-produced.

You were hand-designed.

So was everyone else.

What if we saw each other this way?

Pause & Ponder

Pause in your purple chair or wherever you find stillness. Take three gentle breaths.

Ponder and imagine seeing everyone, including yourself, through this Divine lens.

Who have I overlooked today that bears this Sacred design?

When have I forgotten that I am a gem in God's eyes?

What will shift if I look for the *very good* in everyone I meet?

Prayer

Divine Creator,

You formed me uniquely, exquisitely, and elegantly.

Remind me today that I am not only created in Your image, but so is every single person I encounter.

Give me eyes to see the gems around me— even the ones that are hard to see.

May I live from this truth

And walk gently among Your masterpieces.

Amen & Amen

Journal Invitation

List five people who are easy to love—and five who are not. For each, write one way they reflect God's unique and elegant design. No matter how small, let it shine.

Proceed...

Ripple 3

The Great Gift of Belovedness

Gather

I have loved you with an everlasting love; I have drawn you with unfailing kindness.

— Jeremiah 31:3 (NIV 2011)

For I am convinced that neither death nor life, neither angels or demons, neither the present or the future, nor any powers, neither height nor depth, nor anything else in all creation will be able to separate us from the love of God that is in Christ Jesus.

— Romans 8:38–39 (NRSV)

Reflecting on the Human Struggle

We live in a world that teaches us to earn— affection, approval, acceptance.

So it's no wonder that our hearts, in their earth-suited form, find it hard to take in the kind of love that just *is*.

We try.

We perform, we strive, we serve, we fix, we figure. But still, we ache.

Could it be that the ache isn't for more *doing*, but more *receiving*?

Because the truth is, we are already loved. Not because of what we've done.

Not because of how perfectly we've performed. But because of **who we are.**

I am I.

And I am called *Beloved.*

Illumined by The Divine Contrast

There is a love that cannot be earned. There is a love that cannot be lost.

There is a love that will not leave, no matter how long we run, or how many layers we wear to hide.

It is *everlasting.*

And it is not a distant theology. It's a present truth. We are not on a journey to *become* beloved.

We are on a journey to remember that we *already are.*

The task of our life—our healing, our becoming whole, our returning to true self — is not toward belovedness. It flows **from** it.

Pause & Ponder

Pause and breathe here. Listen.

Let the whisper settle in your heart:

"Nothing can separate you from My love."

Let these questions settle softly in your soul:

- Do I believe I am already beloved—just as I am, here and now?

- Where in my life am I striving to *earn* what I already *have*?

- How would my life shift if I began with belovedness instead of trying to reach for it?

Prayer

Oh Beloved One,

You loved me before I knew how to love.

You call me yours, without condition.

You see through my masks and still call me by name—*Beloved*.

Let this truth seep into my bones.

Let it reframe my story.

Let it soften every striving.

And may my life begin—again and again—from the great gift of belovedness.

Amen & Amen

Journal Invitation

Write a letter from God to you. Begin with:

"My beloved child…"

Let the words come from stillness, not effort.

Then, write a response from your heart—no editing, just honesty.

Proceed...

Ripple 4

Light Bearers Begin Within

Gather

Let your light so shine before others, that they may see your good works and glorify your Father in heaven.

— Matthew 5:16 (NKJV)

Reflecting on the Human Struggle

There's a kind of weariness that creeps in when we try to be light *for everyone else* without tending to the flicker within ourselves. We pour out kindness, patience, attention—while ignoring the shadows that have settled quietly inside.

Sometimes, we think being a "light bearer" means performing brightness—smiling while crumbling, glowing while growing tired.

But true light doesn't come from pretending. It comes from *presence,* from tending the flame within, even when it's barely a spark.

The call to shine doesn't begin in public. It begins in the quiet, sacred work of inner illumination.

Illumined by the Divine Contrast

God never asks us to shine from an empty soul. The light we bear is borrowed—ignited by Divine presence, sustained by grace.

Jesus says, *You are the light*—not because of your perfection, but because of His presence within you. This light isn't forced; it flows. It begins not with output, but with inner stillness.

To bear light, you must first behold it.

When we begin within—nurturing peace, truth, rest, healing—we become radiant. Not flashy. Not loud.

Just lit by Love.

Pause & Ponder

Breathe in: The light begins within.

Breathe out: I shine from Presence, not performance.

Let the glow settle inward.

- Am I trying to be light for others while neglecting my own inner light?
- What does it look like to *begin within*?
- Where do I need tending, so I can shine authentically?

Prayer

Oh Ultimate Source of Light, I come to You not to perform, but to be transformed. Kindle in me the flame of peace, of truth, of holy radiance. Let me tend to the quiet glow of Your Spirit within me, that I may shine not from striving, but from stillness. Make me a light bearer— not despite my shadows, but in the midst of them.

Amen & Amen

Journal Invitation

Where do I desire to let Divine light tend to me today?

What shadows have I been avoiding?

What would it feel like to shine from my true self—from the inside out?

Proceed...

Ripple 5

Sitting in Serenity

Gather

You will keep in perfect peace all who trust in you, all whose thoughts are fixed on you.

— Isaiah 26:3 (NLT)

Reflecting on the Human Struggle

Serenity can feel elusive—like something reserved for the mystics or the monks, tucked away in quiet monasteries far from email and headlines and deadlines.

We want peace, but instead we rehearse our worries. We spiral through to-do lists. We try to *earn* rest by finishing everything first—and rest never comes.

But what if serenity isn't something we *get to* only when life cooperates? What if serenity is something we sit in—something we *practice*, even in the middle of life's swirl? Even in the center of neuro-cycloning?

To sit in serenity is not to escape, but to anchor, To place ourselves in stillness not because the world is calm, but because we refuse to let the storm set our rhythm.

Illumined the Divine Contrast

God's peace is not passive. It is powerful. It guards hearts. It steadies minds. It transcends understanding—not because it ignores the pain, but because it holds us within it.

Serenity isn't the same as apathy. It's a deep, aware, awakened calm—born not of avoidance but of alignment.

We sit in serenity not by numbing out, but by tuning in—fixing our thoughts on the One who keeps us in perfect peace.

This is a holy practice. An awareness of chaos. A release. A return to Presence. Coherence. A Holy Rhythm.

Pause & Ponder

Breathe in: *You will keep me in peace.*

Breathe out: *My mind is fixed on You.*

Let the serenity become a seat for your soul.

What does *serenity* look and feel like to you?

Where do you feel unrest?

What if you could sit *with* that unrest, rather than fight it—and find peace in the sitting?

Prayer

God of Stillness, I long for serenity—not the kind the world offers, but the kind that only You can breathe into my bones. Quiet my racing thoughts. Calm my inner noise. Teach me to sit in serenity, even when life swirls around me. Let Your peace settle over me like a gentle covering. I open myself to You.

Amen & Amen

Journal Invitation

Where in my life do I need serenity right now?

What thoughts or distractions keep pulling me out of stillness?

What would it mean to sit—truly sit—in peace today?

Proceed...

Ripple 6

Purple Chair Pause
A Prayer in the Face of Division

Gather

If it is possible, as far as it depends on you, live at peace with everyone.

— Romans 12:18

Reflecting on the Human Struggle

Division can show up like a chasm between hearts—fueled by wounds, words, weariness, and the ache to be understood. We want to bridge it, fix it, *make* the other person see.

And sometimes peace feels impossible. Conversations fracture. Relationships fumble. Families fray.

In these moments, we sit—not in defeat, but in pause. We breathe—not in avoidance, but in surrender.

We choose to let serenity anchor us before we try to act.

This is the Purple Chair Pause:

A seat of stillness in a divided world.

A moment to remember who we are—not in reaction to others, but in alignment with Love.

Illumined by the Divine Contrast

God does not demand that we *force* peace. But we are called to embody it—*as far as it depends on us.* That begins within.

Jesus met division with presence. He asked questions. He retreated to pray. He spoke truth in love and held boundaries with grace.

In Him, we find our model. In Him, we find the courage to be light in the midst of the storm.

As we pause—in purple chairs or quiet cars or silent prayers—we reclaim our capacity to respond rather than react. We become grounded peace-bringers, not chaos-carriers.

Pause & Ponder

Breathe in: *I choose stillness.*

Breathe out: *I choose peace.*

Let the pause become a holy presence.

Where am I experiencing division right now—internally or externally?

What does it look like to "live at peace" as far as it depends on *me*?

How can I be a vessel of unity rather than division?

Am I reacting from fear or responding from love?

Prayer

Oh Uniting God, I sit in this purple chair—this place of peace—asking You to meet me here. You see the rifts. The tension. The things I cannot fix.

Teach me not to carry condemnation, but compassion. Not judgment, but curiosity.

Make me a bearer of light, beginning within.

And in every space of division, plant in me the seeds of unity and peace.

Amen & Amen

Journal Invitation

What would it look like for me to "live at peace" today?

Where can I pause, breathe, and choose love—even in the face of difference or disconnection?

Proceed...

Ripple 7

Spelunking into the Soul:
Rediscovered

Gather

Be still, and know that I am God.

— Psalm 46:10

Reflecting on the Human Struggle

There comes a time when we realize: We cannot "spelunk" into someone else's soul. Not even for love. Not even for fear. Not even when we see the cliff they don't see, or feel the ache they won't name.

This is especially hard when it's someone we cherish—a son, a daughter, a friend, a partner. We watch them wrestle or resist, and everything in us wants to light the path, carve the tunnel, ease their descent. But the sacred work of "soul spelunking" is personal. Inner work cannot be outsourced.

It's here we face a crossroads: Will we release them? Not in apathy or abandonment, but in deep respect for their journey and their timing; trusting their own encounter with the Divine.

Illumined by the Divine Contrast

"Be still and know…"—not "fix and figure out."

Stillness is active trust.

God "spelunks" with each of our loved ones. The Spirit goes to the depths we dare not tread alone. And sometimes, the holiest offering we can make is to stop interfering with God's work and start interceding—not with pressure, but with presence. Not with control, but with compassion.

To release someone is to honor their soul's sacred dignity—and to trust that God is already there.

As we descend inward ourselves, we become less desperate to manage anyone else's descent. We find a grounded-ness that frees both us *and* them.

Pause & Ponder

Breathe in: *God is already there.*

Breathe out: *I release them in love.*

Breathe in: God is already here.

Breathe out: I release myself into that love.

Feel the space open within you.

- Is there someone I'm trying to "fix," rather than trust God with?

- What happens in me when I consider releasing them—not out of indifference, but in reverent love?

- What might my own soul need in this season of letting go?

- What does my own "spelunking" reveal to me?

Prayer

God of the Deep, You know the caverns of every soul. You know the terrain I cannot reach, even in those I love most. Help me to let go— not in resignation, but in reverent trust. Let my stillness become an offering. Let my surrender become sacred. And while You spelunk into their soul, spelunk into mine too. I am here. I am listening.

Amen & Amen

Journal Invitation

Who am I being invited to release today?

What would it look like to trust God with their soul—and tend gently to my own?

How could I "spelunk" into my own depths? and find me? my essence?

Proceed...

Ripple 8

Wonky and the Way Back

Gather

He restores my soul. He leads me in paths of righteousness for His name's sake.

— Psalm 23:3 (NKJV)

Reflecting on the Human Struggle

Sometimes, there's no better word than *wonky*. That off-center, slightly off-kilter sense—not fully broken, but not quite right. You're not spiraling, but you're not grounded either. You feel disoriented inside your own life.

It might come on suddenly, or sneak up slowly. A conversation rattled you. A memory surfaced. A series of small things finally tipped the scale. The heart doesn't always know why it's out of rhythm. It just is.

In this space, we often try to fix the feeling. To muscle our way back into productivity or calm.

But there's wisdom in pausing, in letting the soul whisper before we try to force it silent.

Illumined by the Divine Contrast

What if the way back isn't about controlling the chaos, but letting yourself be gently led?

The Psalm doesn't say, *"He tells me to pull it together."*

It says, *"He restores my soul."*

This is not self-effort alone. This is surrender. A divine recalibration.

The Good Shepherd doesn't push. He *leads.* And the path is not one of shame, but of righteousness... *for His name's sake.* In other words, our restoration is not a burden to God. His joy, His identity, His promise.

When we're wonky, He's still steady.

Pause & Ponder

Close your eyes. Breathe deeply. Imagine your soul as a compass needle, gently pulled back to center—not by effort, but by nearness to God's presence.

- Where in your life do you feel off-center right now?

- Can you name the sensation, or do you just feel the wonkiness?

- What does it mean to let God *restore* your soul instead of striving to fix it yourself?

Prayer

God of Still Waters,

I admit it: I feel off. Something inside me is wobbly, and I don't quite know how to fix it. But You are the Shepherd Who restores. Lead me gently. Calm my inner waves. I yield to Your rhythm instead of my own urgency. Thank You for not rushing me back to center, but instead walking with me there.

Amen & Amen

Journal Invitation

What does "wonky" look like for me?

What's one small step toward allowing God to restore my soul today?

Proceed...

Ripple 9

When Our Bones Sing
a.k.a. The Resonance Within

Gather

Then he said to me, "Prophesy to these bones and say to them, 'Dry bones, hear the word of the Lord!'"

— Ezekiel 37:4

My heart and flesh sing for joy to the living God.

— Psalm 84:2b

Reflecting on the Human Struggle

We so often try to know God through intellect, seeking answers and explanations that fit inside our human understanding. But God is not confined to logic or speech. Our **earth-suit minds** were never built to hold the vastness of the **Ineffable One**.

We long to hear, to speak, to understand. And yet the deeper language—one of stillness, resonance, and presence—can feel elusive in our noisy world. We may feel spiritually voiceless or deaf to Divine communication. We may forget that there is a **deeper remembering**, even when words fail.

Illumined by the Divine Contrast

God doesn't need our perfect understanding. God meets us in the **marrow**. In the silence. In the resonance that hums beneath language.

From within us, a song rises—not made of melody or verse, but of sacred recognition. A communion so deep it bypasses thought.

Even when we cannot speak, our bones *sing*. Even when we cannot hear, our soul *resonates*. Even in our limitation, **we are known and heard**.

God is within.

God is *with*.

And God is *wordless love*.

Pause & Ponder

Let yourself fall into the stillness. Let your bones begin to remember.

- Have I been trying to figure out God with only my mind?

- What does it mean to listen **with the soul** instead of the ears?

- Where do I feel divine resonance in my body—my chest, my bones, my breath?

Prayer

Holy One Who sings in the silence, meet me in the marrow of my being.

Let me stop trying to understand You with my mind, and begin to encounter You with my soul.

When I cannot speak, sing through me. When I cannot hear, hum within me.

When I forget, remind me that I am known. Even my bones carry the sound of Your love.

Amen & Amen

Journal Invitation

What does my soul want to sing today, without words?

Where do I sense God speaking *beneath* the noise?

How have I experienced resonance in silence?

_____

_____

_____

_____

_____

_____

_____

Proceed...

Ripple 10

Sanctuary from Shenanigans
A purple chair pause in a chaotic world

Gather

Then, because so many people were coming and going that they did not even have a chance to eat, he said to them, "Come with me by yourselves to a quiet place and get some rest." Mark 6:31 (NIV) "Jesus literally invites a retreat, a sanctuary, a pause in the chaos, amidst the shenanigans." KSE

Reflecting on the Human Struggle

The world swirls with noise—distractions, posturing, chaos, and contradictions. So much *activity* disguises itself as importance.

So many *shenanigans*—mischief masquerades as meaning.

In our relationships, in the news, in our own thoughts, there's a constant temptation to perform, to posture, to judge, to react.

We are tugged by drama, baited by fear, seduced by spectacle.

We lose ourselves in the scramble.

And the soul aches for a Sacred hush.

Illumined by the Divine Contrast

But then...

Stillness whispers.

The Spirit breathes.

Christ calls not from the center of the crowd, but from the quiet hill, the garden at night, the boat rocked by wind.

God is never in a rush.

Never in a spin.

Never in the shenanigans.

The Trinity offers sanctuary from the spinning— a return to truth, a re-rooting in Love, a re-membering of what is real.

Pause & Ponder

Pause and Whisper this into your own heart:

"I don't have to join the shenanigans. I am safe in the stillness."

- What "shenanigans" are swirling around me—or within me?
- Where am I reacting instead of resting?

- What if I could retreat without running away—by sitting still and becoming more present?
- What might happen if I made stillness my default instead of distraction?

Prayer

O Still and Steady One,

This world spins and pulls,

but You remain.

You are not in the frenzy,

but in the whisper.

Let me find refuge in You.

Let my heart be a sanctuary

from the noise,

from the chaos,

from the endless proving.

Thank You for the sacred pause,

the silent space,

This purple chair,

This Sanctuary -

where You meet me

with nothing but love.

Amen & Amen.

Journal Invitation

- What "shenanigans" am I tempted to entertain today—externally or internally?

- How do I recognize the difference between playful joy and distracting chaos?

- What does my sanctuary look and feel like? How can I carry it within me, even when the world swirls?

Proceed...

Ripple 11

A Message From This Purple Chair to Yours

Gather

"Peace I leave with you; my peace I give you. I do not give to you as the world gives. Do not let your hearts be troubled and do not be afraid."

—John 14:27 (NIV)

Reflecting on the Human Struggle

We live in a world full of noise—decisions, devices, disappointments, demands.

It's easy to forget that beneath the chaos, something still speaks. The soul longs for a place where we can finally *exhale.*

You sit in the chair—the one you've come to know as Sacred—and even though the world hasn't changed, something in you begins to soften. This chair doesn't ask for your performance. It welcomes your presence. It reminds you that you're not alone.

Still, we resist silence. We fear what we might find if we truly pause. The heart races with all the things left undone. But in this sacred space, there's a deeper invitation:

What if peace is already present? What if you don't have to go find it—only return to it?

Illumined by the Divine Contrast

Jesus speaks to His friends before chaos erupts—and He gives them *peace,* not the kind the world offers—which is temporary, transactional, and fragile—but His own peace.

A peace that transcends stormy conditions.

That's the message from this purple chair: *You don't have to wait for life to calm down to know calm inside.*

The Divine whispers: *Peace is not the absence of trouble; it's the presence of Me.*

This is not self-soothing. This is soul-stilling—a return to the deep breath of God.

Pause & Ponder

Try this: Sit quietly in your own sacred space.

Breathe in: *Peace I give you.*

Breathe out: *Not as the world gives ...*

Let the message of stillness settle within you.

- When was the last time you allowed yourself to simply be still?

- What messages do you hear when you finally quiet the noise?

- Can you imagine a peace that isn't dependent on circumstances?

Prayer

Jesus,

You model and offer a peace this world can't imitate. In the swirl of uncertainty, remind me of Your steady voice. Let my heart be quieted not by control, but by connection. Let this purple chair become holy ground where I meet You—again and again. Let Your peace whisper louder than the chaos.

Amen & Amen

Journal Invitation

What message do I hear when I sit in stillness?

What might God be saying to me today from my own purple chair?

_____

_____

_____

_____

_____

_____

Proceed...

Ripple 12

The Book Ends: In All Things, Love

Gather

The Spirit of the Lord God is upon me, because the Lord has anointed me; he has sent me to bring good news to the oppressed, to bind up the broken hearted, to proclaim liberty to the captives, and release to the prisoners, to proclaim the year of the Lord's favor...

— Isaiah 61:1–2a (NRSV)

"In All things - Love.

In Essentials - Unity.

In Non-essentials - Liberty.

In All things - Love."

—From the Moravian Motto

Reflecting on the Human Struggle

Sometimes, I feel the weight of these words more personally than I expect:

Oppressed.   Brokenhearted.   Captive. Prisoner.

They are not just as distant descriptors of others, but echoes in my own soul.

Tied up by the culture. Caught by my own biases. Adrift in the confusion and noise.

And I know I'm not alone. These are shared human aches.

I hear the ache in the conversations around me. I see it in weary eyes. We are not always free, even when we think we are.

And sometimes we forget that Love is the starting point, not the reward.

Illumined by the Divine Contrast

And yet...

There it is again.

The whisper:

"In all things, Love."

In essentials, unity. In non-essentials, liberty.

And in *all things,* Love.

I lean into Isaiah's vision and feel the pulse of God's invitation:

- **Bring the good news.** The good news that we are beloved. Image-bearers. Designed to reflect light. We are the plan....

- **Bind up the brokenhearted.** I looked up "bind up." It means more than bandaging. It means embracing, wrapping with strength, holding with compassion. A soul-hug.

- **Proclaim liberty.** Freedom planted deep within by a delighting God. It's always been there, just hidden under layers of noise, fear, shame.

This isn't just poetic. It's a pattern. It's rhythmic.

This is how Love Ripples out - Abounds.... Overflows....

Pause & Ponder

Take a moment. Take a deep breath,

- Where do you feel captive right now?
- What needs binding—with compassion, not correction?
- What is your good news to carry today?
- How can love ripple from you toward one soul in need?
- What would it mean to live today as if Isaiah 61 was already happening in you, around you, and through you?

Prayer

Loving God,

Whisper again the good news over my heart. Let me see where I am still bound...

Let me see, not with shame, but with curiosity and grace.

Bind up my weary places with your embrace.

And help me ripple love outward—in essentials with unity, in differences with liberty, and in all things with Love.

Amen & Amen.

Journal Invitation

What does it look like for me to love myself as one who is beloved—and then let that love ripple outward?

Where do I long for unity that still honors liberty?

Proceed...

Closing Blessing
A Whisper at the End

You have traveled gently through these ripples—not rushing, not forcing, simply letting each one meet you as it may.

And now, as you rise from this purple chair or close the final page, may this blessing go with you...

A Whisper at the End

May you remember that you are not alone.

Even when it feels like no one sees,

You are fully known.

Even when it feels like no one hears,

You are deeply understood.

Even when it feels like no one stays,

You are forever held.

There is a Presence within you,

A light that cannot be dimmed.

It is not earned.

It cannot be lost.

It simply *is*.

And it has been with you.

All along.

May this knowing ripple into your days.

May peace accompany your thoughts.

May love rise like breath from your soul.

And the next time you feel alone,

May you feel instead *Accompanied.*

Journal Invitation

Before this journey ends, take a few quiet minutes to write, reflect, or simply sit in sacred stillness: Write your own Epilogue.

What has stirred in you through these ripples?

What are you carrying differently now?

What does Presence feel like in your body right now?

_____

_____

_____

From This Purple Chair to Yours

with Gratefulness, Joy, Peace, Faith, Hope, and Love

This page is lovingly and intentionally left blank for you. To listen.

To breathe.

To simply be.

To rest into the truth that you are beloved and uniquely, exquisitely and elegantly created by the Designer of designers.

Thought-Life Invitations
From This Purple Chair to You

Pause... Sacred Ground:

The Liminal spaces between stimulus and reaction; old perspective and new perspective, old thought and new thought happen in the Pause.

Go there. Take a breath. Release. And Return.

Speak to yourself always with TLC^3: Tender Loving Care, Compassion, and Curiosity.

Lean into curiosity rather than judgement, blame, shame, guilt or condemnation.

Remember: Awareness is not punishment - it is possibility.

It is Key.

You are uniquely, exquisitely, and elegantly designed.

Beloved from the beginning to the end of time....

and beyond.

And be reminded, sweet friend, You're Not Alone.

If you're creating, recovering, growing,

or simply breathing your way back to yourself.

You're not behind. You're not broken.

You're in motion.

And the ripples you're creating

are more beautiful than you know.

A Resource Guide

Welcome Fellow Traveler!

If you've landed here, you're likely a fellow seeker, a quiet ponderer, a deep feeler—someone who listens for the whispers beneath the noise. This guide is a gentle offering from one traveler to another—sharing tools, truths, and treasures that have supported me on this path of creativity, healing, and soulful thought-life coaching.

Creative Companions and Tools

- This Naked Mind & The Alcohol Experiment by Annie Grace:

These teachings helped me find freedom—not only from alcohol, but from toxic thinking and limiting beliefs. A new way of seeing, with compassion and curiosity at the center.

https://thisnakedmind.com   https://thisnakedmind.com/the-alcohol-experiment

- ChatGPT by OpenAI: My digital companion—part assistant, part muse, part interpreter, part administrative assistant— helped me shape language, structure, and flow for many of my reflections.

Learn more: https://chat.openai.com

A Note About Tools Like ChatGPT

Many people wonder whether using AI in soul work is appropriate. Here's what I've discovered: when used intentionally and ethically, ChatGPT is like a pen that listens. It reflects, refines, and helps me say more clearly what my heart already knows. There is no cost beyond my subscription, no ownership claim over my work. Just a quiet, helpful presence— one ripple among many.

Books, Voices, and Verses That Stirred and Inspired My Soul

- The Message Bible – Eugene Peterson
- The Renovare Bible
- The Book of Awakening - Mar Nepo
- Everything Belongs, Falling Upward, Eager to Love – Richard Rohr
- Pollyanna, the movie – Eleanor H. Porter (and her pastor's wisdom!)
- The Way to Love - Anthony de Mello
- Interior Castle by Teresa of Avila
- Julian of Norwich
- This Naked Mind by Annie Grace
- The Map of Consciousness Explained, Force vs. Power, Letting Go by Dr. David Hawkins
- Henri Nouwen

Scripture References

Scripture quotations throughout this devotional respite are drawn from a variety of translations, each chosen for its clarity, beauty, and resonance with the heart of these reflections. The words of Scripture have been selected with care—from versions that speak both tenderly and truthfully to the soul. Versions used include the NIV (1984 & 2011), NKJV, NASB, NLT, NRSV, and The Message.

Glossary

Awareness

Awareness is the practice of noticing one's thoughts, emotions, and surroundings with openness and clarity.

It is the first step toward conscious living and choice, allowing an individual to respond rather than react to life.

Belovedness

Belovedness is the recognition of one's inherent value and worth in the eyes of God.

It is the truth that each person is loved unconditionally and forever, forming the foundation for confidence, compassion, and spiritual growth.

Companioning the Other

Companioning the Other is the practice of walking alongside another person on their spiritual, emotional, or thought-life journey.

In my work, I serve as a spiritual companion and thought-life coach, walking with fellow travelers with presence, curiosity, and tender support — never directing or controlling their path. I walk beside them, holding space for their emotional and spiritual "batteries," offering encouragement, hope, and relationship.

Through this practice, I provide tools, insights, and gentle tactics to help my fellow traveler notice their inner patterns, explore choices, and cultivate awareness — always in a way that honors their autonomy and unique journey.

Companioning the other is about creating a sacred space where they can discover their own wisdom, freedom, and alignment with God's guidance. It is a tender partnership, honoring both their human struggle and their capacity to live into their divine essence.

Companioning the Self

Companioning the Self is the practice of approaching one's own inner life with curiosity, tenderness, and presence.

It involves listening without judgment, offering understanding, and walking gently alongside one's thoughts, feelings, and experiences.

Devotional

A devotional is a short, reflective reading or practice intended to focus the heart and mind on God.

In this book, devotionals are often referred to as "ripples," because each one is designed to create an effect that spreads outward — gently influencing awareness, thought, and spiritual reflection.

See also: Ripple.

Divine Contrast

The divine contrast is the sacred shift from our earth-bound struggle into our deeper essence—the part of us held in God, shaped by Christ, and breathed by the Spirit.

It is the movement from the swirl of our thoughts and reactions into the quiet, steady truth of who we are in God, The Divine.

The divine contrast is illustrated in my practice by the lighting of three candles, gently marking the movement from human struggle into essence living—a reminder that God's presence is spacious, steady, and sustaining. It is a movement into trust, love, and awareness, without erasing our humanity.

Human Struggle

The human struggle is the honest, everyday experience of living life in our "earth suits" — our beautiful, vulnerable humanity.

It includes the longings, limitations, reactions, patterns, wounds, hopes, and emotions that arise simply because we are human.

Human struggle is not a failure; it is an invitation to awareness and growth. Naming the human struggle is an act of compassion and honesty, recognizing the soil from which transformation and freedom emerge.

Meta-Ripple

Meta means going beyond what is happening to notice, name, and choose the thoughts beneath it. A Meta Ripple is a ripple of awareness—the sacred space where we pause, ponder and pray.

This cognitive spiritual work, this meta-ripple, clarifies and brings greater light. Meta carries the sense of "transformation," which is precisely what happens in spiritual companioning and thought-life work.

Neuro-cycloning

Neuro-cycloning is the mental process of looping through the same thoughts, stories, fears, or beliefs over and over again—often without awareness.

It is what happens when the mind spins in familiar patterns shaped by past experiences, old narratives, or subconscious scripts. Neuro-cycloning can feel like being swept into an inner swirl, where the same thought keeps circling without bringing clarity, peace, or resolution.

In my work, naming neuro-cycloning is an act of compassion—a way of bringing the pattern into awareness so it can be gently interrupted, observed, and transformed. When we pause, notice, and breathe, the cycle loosens and space opens for curiosity, choice, and freedom.

Paraphrase

A paraphrase is a restating of Scripture in fresh, contemporary language while preserving the heart and meaning of the original passage.

It is not a direct quotation or formal translation, but a way of expressing biblical truth through one's own voice, experience, and understanding.

In this book, a paraphrase serves as a bridge —connecting the ancient wisdom of Scripture with the lived, everyday language of spiritual formation. When I paraphrase a verse, I am listening closely to its intent and offering it in words that feel accessible, compassionate, and resonant. A paraphrase honors the text while also honoring the human heart that longs to understand it.

Ponder

To ponder is to sit and offer yourself space and time to just listen.

Pondering is not overthinking, but a slow, spacious listening. It invites reflection on thoughts, emotions, Scripture, or moments of life, allowing insight, wisdom, and understanding to emerge.

Purple Chair Pause

A Purple Chair Pause is a moment of stillness and reflection inspired by sitting in my own purple chair.

It is a gentle invitation to slow down, notice, and bring attention to one's thoughts, feelings, and relationship with God. These pauses are spaces of awareness, grounding, and reorientation.

Ripple

A ripple is a short meditation, reflection, or practice designed to spread insight, awareness, or spiritual truth outward from a single moment.

Like ripples in water, the effects extend beyond the initial point, inviting the reader to notice, reflect, and respond.

In this book, ripples are the same as "respite" devotionals—short reflections created to usher in rest, spark awareness, pause, and spiritual growth. While the term "devotional" describes the traditional practice, "ripple" reflects the gentle, spreading effect each reflection has on the mind, heart, and spirit.

See also: Devotional.

Spelunking

Spelunking, in the spiritual and emotional sense, is the practice of courageously exploring the inner caverns of the soul.

It is a descent into the hidden spaces of the heart—thoughts, memories, patterns, beliefs, and longings—not to fix or judge, but to understand and lovingly attend to what we find.

This inner spelunking is always done with tenderness and compassion, trusting that God meets us in the depths. It is a journey of re-discovery, release, and return: exploring what is beneath the surface, letting go of what no longer serves, and emerging with greater clarity, compassion, and alignment with our true essence; our wholeness.

The Director's Chair

The Director's Chair is a metaphor for placing oneself in a position of conscious choice over one's thoughts, feelings, and actions.

Sitting in this chair allows the individual to observe, guide, and shape the inner life with awareness and compassion.

Three Candle Practice

A spiritual practice that I have routinized. I use it to prepare, to settle, orient, and center oneself before reflection, companioning, or prayer.

The Three Candle Practice is a gentle, tangible way of marking sacred space and reminding both mind and heart of the truths one chooses to live by. When entering the purple chair, three candles are lit: one in the name of God the Creator (Father), one in the name of the Messiah who loves life (Son), and one in the name of the Spirit who fuels life (Spirit). These candles are not meant to confine or explain God; they simply help touch something of God's vast, indescribable presence, creating a pause that settles the mind, centers the heart, and invites awareness—a doorway into the divine contrast, moving from earth-suit living into the essence of who we are in God. If you are more comfortable with language that is broader, you may choose to light one candle in honor of creation, one in honor of unconditional love and one in honor or the fuel for life.

Thought-life

Thought-life is the totality of our conscious and subconscious thinking—the stream of ideas, judgments, memories, and imaginings that influence how we feel, act, and respond to life.

In this book, cultivating a healthy thought-life is central to freedom, awareness, and transformation.

Trinity

The Trinity is the Christian understanding of God as Father, Son (Messiah), and Spirit—three persons who together reveal something of God's infinite being.

For me, the Trinity was never meant to box God in. I believe these three "persons" are not limits on who God is, but windows into His vast, indescribable nature. They help me name and feel aspects of God's presence in my life while remembering that God is far greater than any words, concepts, or human explanations. The Trinity is a doorway into relationship, not a cage, offering a living, sustaining, and deeply personal reality.

Acknowledgments with Gratitude

With much love to all my fellow travelers:

You know who you are. You are old friends and new friends and treasured family who have traveled with me on this path we call life on earth.

I am grateful for my circle of friends for their encouragement, support, wisdom, and love: Kim Denyes, Stephanie Emeigh, Janet Pressler, Kimberly Torcaso, Nesha Parker, and Barb Schindler. This work would not have happened without them.

To Annie Grace and My Fellow Coaches:

Your stories and your work through This Naked Mind became a beacon of freedom for me—freedom not only from alcohol, but from toxic thinking. Through your voices, I rediscovered the profound truth that we are inherently capable of being free—free from numbing behaviors, substances, and the thought patterns that keep us small. Thank you for helping me rediscover a life of joy and abundance, a life that brims over with hope.

This purple chair is that place of peace for our naked minds.

To my "legacy making" fam:

There are not enough words to describe this family of mine—The Fam:

My adult children, Kurt & Stephanie, Jana, Scott & Kim and Mark & Courtney,

My nine grandchildren: Joshua, Derek, Jackson, Charlie, Idina, James Duke, Landon, Norah, and Dax

My rock, my steady-as-he-goes, my husband, my love, Paul

And our loyal dog, Ollie.

The love and joy you all bring to me and each other is abundant—my heart swells!

You are the fuel that gives me energy and purpose.

*We are leaving a Legacy **together!***

With a deep love, respect, and gratitude, I acknowledge Jennifer Bright and her team at Bright Communications. This book would never have come to fruition without them! It seems like she knew inherently when I was ready to give up, and a note, text, or email would show up or a conversation would be held and she would be that needed source of encouragement and inspiration and the fuel that kept me going. Thank you from the depths of my heart, Jennifer!

About the Author

Welcome to *This Purple Chair*—a place for pause, reflection, and rediscovery. I'm Kathy, and I companion fellow travelers like you, helping you quiet the noise, reconnect with your truest self, and experience a life you don't want to escape from.

But I didn't arrive here overnight.

For years, I believed I was doing "just fine." I kept busy, stayed productive, and did all the right things. But slowly, I found myself leaning on numbing behaviors—especially alcohol—to cope with stress and disconnect. I thought I was in control. I wasn't.

My turning point came in a moment of painful clarity. I was exhausted. Disconnected. And ready for something more. That's when I sat down into my own version of *this purple chair*—a space to listen deeply, explore what was underneath the noise, and return to the uniquely, exquisitely, elegantly designed me.

Now, I help others do the same.

For more information, please visit my website at thispurplechair.com

My Approach

I don't "fix" people—and I don't believe you're broken.

Through spiritual companioning, thought-life coaching, group conversations, and Affective Liminal Psychology™ I support you in:

- Recognizing and quieting your inner critic
- Breaking free from numbing thoughts, behaviors, or substances
- Reconnecting with the vibrant, wise, and free you that's always been there

My credentials include:

- Certified Spiritual Guide
- Certified This Naked Mind AF Coach
- Certified Affective Liminal Psychology™ Coach

- Thought-Life Coach
- Elder at The Gate: A Faith Community Bethlehem PA

Multiple degrees:

- Bachelor of Education from Rider University
- Masters of Speech and Language/ Deaf Education from Pennsylvania State University
- I also have completed post graduate work on teaching and learning from East Stroudsburg University, Arcadia University, and Lehigh University, and I have earned the highest certification in the PA State Education System: Letter of Eligibility

And best of all, I am so thankful and enjoy living life with my husband and our four grown children, their spouses, and our nine grand-children.

Coming Soon! *From This Purple Chair to Yours: Ripples of a New Song*

This Purple Chair

Kathy Emeigh